FEAR

AND

WONDERFULLY
MADE

A Search of the Scriptures for Understanding
Mental and Physical Disabilities

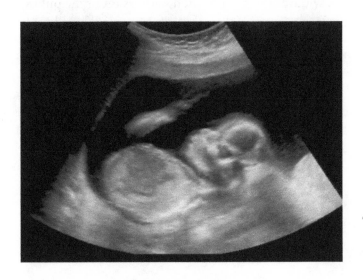

Chenelle Harris

ISBN 978-1-63630-457-1 (Paperback)
ISBN 978-1-63630-458-8 (Digital)

Covenant Books, Inc.
11661 Hwy 707
Murrells Inlet, SC 29576
www.covenantbooks.com

To everyone who the Lord blesses with the opportunity to love and care for a person with a disability, I pray that my journey encourages you.

I thank my daughter, Sydney, for giving me the final push I needed: "I hope you really do something with it. A lot of people need this."

MY JOURNEY

FOREWORD

Minister Cleo Holloway

An excellent spiritual reflection of how our plans are not always congruent with the plan of God. It shows you how to or that it is necessary to realize that our thoughts, beliefs, preconceived notions for self and others must align itself to the true plan and purpose of God.

A life experience that offers solid scripture-based principles that can help believers to survive the challenges, roadblocks, twists, and turns while on what seems to be a perilous journey. How through a process of time and fervent prayer one comes to grasp how what seemed to be an issue, challenge, or even a disappointment was in retrospect part of God's amazing plan.

Chenelle's transparent view provides real-life evidence that supports the belief that unforeseeable events in our lives, emotional dysfunction, hardships, crushing disappointments, and intended faith crushers may attack, but God will help you to stand victoriously and allow you to see the blessing and the beauty of His wonderful creation.

This book depicts a developing relationship with God that catapulted Chenelle into becoming a true woman of faith and a mother who would eventually remove and release her own predefined perception of what perfection looked like, only to discover that God was molding her into becoming perfected by His love toward her, His Grace, and His Mercy.

You will witness the process of transformation in her thinking by reflection and introspection. How authentic love defined the perfect child and the realization that Miles did not need a cure because a cure meant that something was wrong. Praying and waiting for a miracle when God had already performed a miracle and provided her with a blessing from the Lord.

Chenelle has reached the destination of where she can exercise spiritual maturity and solely rely on the Word of God. She is now able to filter her thoughts, trust God completely no matter what and proactively choose to Let God be God, and most importantly, love and nurture Miles and see him through the lenses of an Almighty God. Enjoy the read. You will be inspired.

ACKNOWLEDGMENTS

To my Lord and Savior Jesus Christ, thank you for your grace and mercy towards me.

To my husband, Andre, how blessed we are that God chose us to be Miles's parents. I love you and thank you for being such an awesome father to Miles.

To my daughter, Sydney, thank you for being such a loving sister to your brother.

To my parents, Edward and Gwendolyn East, I really can't find the right words. Your dedication to parenting and grandparenting is evidence of the answer to the question "what would Jesus do?"

To my local and out of state family members and friends, your love and support of Miles confirms that God handpicked you to be a part of our village.

To my Pastor, Walter R. Dean, who passed away on December 20, 2020, and Mrs. Ernestine Dean, thank you for your unwavering faith and love for our family.

To Minister Barbara Adams and the Tidewater Women's Fellowship, thank you for being the first to put my words into print. Your encouragement came at a very dry season in my life. I am so glad you positioned yourself to be used by God.

To Kendra Berry, I just thank God for placing you in Miles's life. I thank you for caring and loving Miles in such an excellent way and fulfilling your divine assignment.

Thank you Marlene Vessells-Austin and Linda Seay for your encouragement and guidance.

INTRODUCTION

I know each day is a new opportunity full of grace and mercy. I know that God forgives. I love the Lord my God with all my heart. I believe that Jesus died so that I might live. I want desperately to live a worthy and honorable life before God.

However, I was tired of questioning and tired of the devil's lies about why my son, Miles, who has or is born with—I have never been comfortable with how I should say it—Down syndrome. There were times that I felt personally responsible for his disability. At times, I have been overcome with fear. Fearful of his future and how the world would treat him. At times, I felt both ways at the same time. With this book, my objective was to search the Word of God for answers, clarity, and peace that only God can provide. I was praying for strength and guidance. I came to Him naked, without shame, just as I was.

I trust and believe in God. He is Alpha and Omega, the beginning and the end. I told Satan that God has a plan. I just couldn't see it yet. I just had to walk in faith. I told Satan, "You had me for a moment, but I was weak. I'm no longer going to focus on you, allow you to stir up my self-pity." I said, "Satan, you are under my feet." Yep, that is what I said, and that is what I continued to say.

But sometimes when (1) I heard a message on healing and God still being in the miracle business, (2) Miles's school reports were not favorable, (3) and when I began to think about Miles and what will happen to him if Andre and I are not around, at those times, I began to struggle.

I began to write this book over ten years ago. My personal anthem was that with this book, I would begin my search for ultimate peace, and that in the Powerful and Matchless name of Jesus, by the time this book is finished and published, I would not be struggling anymore in this area of my life.

I felt that if I did not take the time to express my thoughts, I would remain forever stagnant, incapable of walking in my complete purpose until I moved beyond this questioning, doubting, and fear.

If you picked up this book because you have a child or have a person in your life with a disability, I can't make any guarantees about how you'll feel at the last word of the book. But I do know that if you open your heart and mind and ask God to speak to you, he will. I speak from experience as he was faithful to hear my cry and heal my heart and mind.

Although it has been over ten years since I first started writing this book, I've attempted to make my journey clear by presenting the chapters in their original format.

I'm standing on:

> Ask and it will be given to you; seek and you will find; knock and the door will be opened to you. For everyone who asks receives; he who seeks finds; and to him who knocks, the door will be opened. (Matt. 7:7–8)

> Blessed is the one who reads the words of this prophecy, and blessed are those who hear it and take to heart what is written in it, because the time is near. (Rev. 1:3)

CHAPTER 1

My Plan

On September 1, 1995, Miles Elijah Harris was born. Miles, who we planned for, had his name picked out months before his arrival. Andre and I went to the hospital all set to bring our son into the world. My main concern was making sure I received an epidural—I'm not fond of pain. As I recall, we were the only couple in our Lamaze class not planning for a natural delivery. So due to the expected pain of childbirth, my focus was on pain-relieving medicines and pain-relieving medicines alone.

I honestly don't recall the specific details, but I received my medicine, and at some point, due to Miles having an irregular/elevated heart rate, he had to be delivered by caesarean section. I was not so upset. This meant I was surely not going to have to go through the anticipated labor pains. So off we went and Miles came.

The next evening, due to a sustained high temperature, we were advised that he could not be in the room with me and he had to stay in the nursery. Then on Sunday morning (I often think about the meaning of Sunday morning, but I'll get to that in a moment), Dr. Stephen Bolduc, who I had met one time at an open house "come meet the pediatrician" event, came in and said, "I believe your son has Down syndrome." He begin to indicate signs like his high temperature, the length of his tongue, size of his ears, a line across his hand that ended in the middle, a space between his toes. What?

In my mind, I don't think I said it out loud. I was like, "What? Who are you? Why did I choose you? My son is healthy! You don't know my God. We are Christians. Me and my house, we serve the Lord. HELP!"

We immediately called my pastor, Dr. Walter R. Dean, and my church family for prayer. See, with this situation occurring on Sunday morning, all the saints that we knew, love, and trusted were already in place at God's house. Three of our church members, my Pastor's wife, Mrs. Ernestine Dean, Juanita Smith; and Minister Cleo Holloway, came to the hospital to join us and my parents. We prayed because it changes things. "The effectual fervent prayer of a righteous man availeth much" (James 5:16). I know that the prayers of a lot of my family members sustained me at times when I did not know how to pray, chose not to pray, or was just so blind and confused by the enemy that I just could not pray. I had recommitted my life to God four years prior to Miles's birth, so I could now pray for myself.

But now I'm not sure if we were all praying for the same things in the hospital room that morning. We were all there on one accord. Or were we? I was praying for another diagnosis. But something tells me now that maybe there were also prayers going up for our strength, faith, guidance, and understanding of the parenting journey that had just began for us.

So we prayed and a few weeks later, after a battery of tests, it was confirmed that Miles did have Down syndrome, along with two holes in his heart that would need to be closed as soon as he was able to go through the surgery.

Nothing had prepared me for this. I'm positive that there was not a section in all the pregnancy books about this scenario. What do I do? What does this mean? What happened to our prayers? What did we do? What did I do? That is what I kept thinking to myself. It is also what the devil kept constantly whispering in my ears. It takes a lot of energy and will to drown out the voice of the enemy if you give him your attention.

So I became tired and distracted. Here I am, an active church member desiring to live a positive life, trying so hard to forget my days in the world. Focused on having this life, this marriage, and a family that is pleasing to God. Now, here I am struggling to understand what was happening to me, walking with my head held down at times. Other times, even with my game face on, my heart, spirit, faith were hanging down and hurting bad. Now what? What am I to do? This was not in my plan.

CHAPTER 2

Created by God

There are so many categories. Why do I have to place a label on my son? To this day, there is not one that really makes me comfortable. I've come to the conclusion that categorizing is really for two reasons: (1) monetary funding for proper educational programs, noneducational social programs, etc.; and then (2) explanation, providing a reason or, to be blunt, an excuse for someone's behavior to assist the world in understanding and accepting.

Let's look at some words:

- *Disability* (n.)—"feebleness, incapacity, injury, weakness"
- *Disable* (v.)—"incapacitate, cripple, impair"
- *Retard* (v.)—"hinder, postpone, delay, impede"
- *Special (special need)* (adj.)—"specific, certain, particular, designated, unique, distinctive, uncommon, unusual"
- *Need (special need)* (n.)—"poverty: indigence, penury; lack: shortage, inadequacy; requirement: necessity, requirement"

What is your vote? What would make you comfortable to say? Which one makes you feel better, more politically correct?

Now, let's look at the Word of God:

> For you created my inmost being; you knit me together in my mother's womb. I praise you because I am fearfully and wonderfully made; your works are wonderful, I know that full well. My frame was not hidden from you when I was made in the secret place. When I was woven together in the depths of the earth, your eyes saw my unformed body. All the days ordained for me were written in your book before one of them came to be. (Ps. 139:13–16)

> Before I formed you in the womb, I knew you. (Jer. 1:5)

> This is what the Lord says—your Redeemer, who formed you in the womb; I am the Lord who has made all things." (Isa. 44:24)

These scriptures pertain to everyone, including my son, Miles. If these are all true, then he was carefully planned. He was woven to be just who he is. He was touched by the hands of God while he was yet in the womb. He is not a mystery, something that you or I need to figure out. He is a child of God. He was created by the Creator.

I can see with my physical eyes that there is a difference in Miles. I know that there is a difference in how Miles processes thoughts, how he learns, etc. But that should not be my or your focus when we meet people. We are all made by the hands of God. No matter if there is a skin, gender, height, language, physical, or mental processing difference, God is the Creator.

At times I've been taunted by Satan with the thought that Miles's life is somehow not complete. Thoughts that he would be unable to fulfill any real purpose because of the lack in his life, or more accurately, perceived lack. I have cried many tears while being consumed by these thoughts. But the scriptures above say that God made us all, that He took His time with all of us, that He knew Miles and loved him while he was yet in the womb.

I know we look at persons with disabilities, especially children, and think how much more difficult life is for them. We sometimes feel saddened. Why are they like that? What happened? Well, in Isaiah 44, God says He made all things. So if He made all things and we believe in Him and that He did, then we no longer need to question the value of one life over another. God made us all.

> Through him all things were made; without him nothing was made that has been made. (John 1:3)

So we know that He made us. If I truly believe that, then why still the open questions, pondering and wondering at times about how Miles will fit and make it in this earthly world? The questions and thoughts come because I, and a lot of other people, just genuinely want to know why. We're curious. Some people have careers centered on figuring out how something occurs so that we can understand it better. Or is it because we think if we know *how* and/or *why*, it increases our chances of being able to manipulate, to change the outcome? I also believe that in some cases, we are not meant to understand but just to accept and love.

We know the physical and DNA definition of Down syndrome, but we don't know why it occurs.

> I will destroy the wisdom of the wise; the intelligence of the intelligent I will frustrate. (1 Cor. 1:19)

> The secret things belong to the Lord our God, (Deut. 29:29)

> As you do not know the path of the wind, or how the body is formed in a mother's womb,

so you cannot understand the work of God, the
Maker of all things. (Eccles. 11:5)

We can't fully know all the things of God unless He reveals
them to us.

Samuel did not yet know the LORD: The
word of the LORD had not yet been revealed to
him. (1 Sam. 3:7)

I need to interject here. Not sure if I made it clear, but this journey, this book, is based on my belief that God is Alpha and Omega. He is our creator. I don't doubt that one iota. I don't want anyone to take my weakness for disbelief. I am just in need of God's full armor. I need to put it on and stop taking it off.

Therefore put on the full armor of God, so
that when the day of evil comes, you may be able
to stand your ground, and after you have done
everything, to stand. Stand firm then, with the
belt of truth buckled around your waist, with the
breastplate of righteousness in place, and with
your feet fitted with the readiness that comes
from the gospel of peace. (Eph. 6:13–15)

I want my life to be holy and acceptable to God. But I know that until I have fully cast down the lies of Satan in regards to this area of my life, I will not be truly effective for God here on earth.

By searching the scriptures with an open heart and mind, it has become clear to me. An extra chromosome does not indicate that his life was not created by God. God made Miles, you, me, and all people with or without special needs.

But if I know that fact, why can't I put a period here and end the conversation? Because Satan is busy busy, busy. He said, "Okay, you are right. God made him. But do you know why he is different, why the extra chromosome? It is YOU."

CHAPTER 3

Guilt

Often, during the first few months of Miles's life while we were waiting for him to weigh enough to have open heart surgery, I would sense that Miles would not survive. Why was I feeling that? Was it Satan? We like to blame him. Or was it my own personal fear? Andre and I had committed our marriage and life to God. We were looking for some bumps in the road but not potholes and dead ends. I was feeling so overwhelmed all the time. I think I hid it well, but I was hurting on the inside. A hurt that I now know could not be soothed by others. While two church members, Joyce Bright and Eleanor Harris Mincey, reached out to comfort me prior to his surgeries just when I was sinking into hopelessness, God was the only one that could attend to this type of pain.

Eventually, I moved on to what I call my coping or, now more fitting, my denial phase. My strategy for dealing with my prayers not being answered at that time (note: "not being answered" in my opinion) became *this is not the final answer.* God was going to perform a miracle in this situation. I just had to wait and be patient. Just wait. Just wait you old, devil. You'll see.

Well, more and more challenges occurred. Surgery was required, medical bills piled up, and it became evident that Down syndrome was a part of our lives. Then came the guilt.

I began to create and embrace a cause and effect. This was all due to one of the many sins I had committed in my life. I was sure of it. One time, I even went back to an unkind thing I did when I was around thirteen: essentially making fun of people with mental challenges. If I had been nicer, this would not be happening. I did this to my son. God forgives but there are consequences. This was my consequence.

Ultimately, I could not come to terms with how I caused Miles's diagnosis of Down Syndrome, but Satan did not have to give me specifics, as long as the seed was planted that this was my fault, his work was done. I had given him my attention. I was still going to church. I was still praying for strength and guidance. But because I was also still giving attention to Satan's voice, I did not have peace. I was listening to the enemy, so I could not focus on what God was saying. This is not rocket science. Multitasking is not effective in spiritual things. There are times when we have to stop and listen. Reading the Word, singing the songs, reciting scripture, doing the work of the church are requirements for our growth and development. But sometimes you have to stop and listen to God. Not hearing Him and knowing what He wants for you specifically will lead to a lack of assurance, peace, and ineffectiveness in His kingdom. I was moving, working, praising, fasting, but not listening. I had my game face on, but I was not really in the game. Ever heard of "dry bones"?

> Then he said to me: "Son of man, these bones are the whole house of Israel. They say, 'Our bones are dried up and our hope is gone; we are cut off.' Therefore prophesy and say to them: 'This is what the Sovereign LORD says: O my people, I am going to open your graves and bring you up from them; I will bring you back to the land of Israel. Then you, my people, will know that I am the LORD, when I open your graves and bring you up from them. I will put my Spirit in you and you will live, and I will settle you in your own land. Then you will know that I the LORD have spoken, and I have done it, declares the LORD.'" (Ezek. 37:11–14)

This is where I was for a long time. I love Miles. I have a mother's love for him like I should. Yet I have also had this battle going on within me. A battle which says I was responsible, that his life was a consequence of something I had done—GUILT. A guilt so consuming that I was unable to really embrace and focus in on the Word of God. I was walking, working, smiling, singing, praying but all the while feeling so, so guilty. Guilt can be defined as a cognitive or an emotional experience that occurs when a person realizes or believes, accurately or not, that he or she has violated a moral standard and bears significant responsibility for that violation.

Now, there are absolutely things in my life that I am guilty of. There are things I've said, done, not done, and thought about that directly violate my values and the Word of God. I am guilty as charged in a lot of things over my forty-plus years (remember, I wrote this a while ago). See, I know without a doubt that grace, mercy, and forgiveness work overtime for me in all areas of my life. I have been blessed in my life beyond what I had ever imagined. Not just dreams achieved but blessings that were undeserved. I had and do proclaim that it has been the mighty move of God. Yet when it comes to Miles and his disability, there are times when I just feel so defeated.

CHAPTER 4

While Yet in the Womb

> As he went along, he saw a man blind from birth. His disciples asked him, Rabbi, who sinned, this man or his parents, that we was born blind? Neither this man nor his parents sinned, said Jesus, but this happened so that the work of God might be displayed in his life. (John 9:1–3)

I wish I could find the words to express how this scripture comforts me. I know what you are thinking, *Is she saying she is without sin?* Absolutely not! I'm a product of a whole lot of grace and mercy. But sometimes when I give way to the enemy and find myself in a bad place, this scripture has an uplifting effect. However, this scripture has multiple facets. First, as you grow closer to the Lord, it is real evident that He is not a "I'm going to make you pay" kind of God. He does instruct and lead, but He is not a recorder of wrongdoings. He does not make you live with a cloud over your head or walk around with a "sinner" T-shirt.

> He makes them listen to correction and commands them to repent of their evil. If they obey and serve him, they will spend the rest of their days in prosperity and their years in contentment. (Job 36:10–11)

He will forgive you of your sins if you ask him.

> Repent then, and turn to God, so that your
> sins may be wiped out, that times of refreshing
> may come from the Lord. (Act 3:19)

What this scripture is telling us is that the man being born blind is not a direct effect of his parents' actions. We have to stop blaming ourselves and having pity on our children. This negative thinking only hinders us from providing our children with what they need. I am not saying that there are not situations that appear to have a true cause and effect. Smoking, poor nutrition, and drug use will probably have a negative impact on a child at birth. But not everything can be tangible and linked. Some matters require spiritual wisdom.

> For this reason, since the day we heard
> about you, we have not stopped praying for you
> and asking God to fill you with the knowledge of
> his will through all spiritual wisdom and under-
> standing. (Col. 1:9)

Second, I remember I went from denial of my son's condition to "I'm waiting for the miracle." The tests were going to indicate that he does not have Down's. But then I went to "He has Down syndrome, but he will not show any of the traits. The miracle is coming. It's coming. It's coming. I'm waiting. I'm waiting. I'm waiting." But nothing happened. Then I read this scripture that says, "But this happened so that the work of God might be displayed in his life."

God did not have to remove the traits to perform His purpose in Miles's life. The Word is displayed in his life. How powerful is that revelation? I have missed precious time waiting for God to remove something. When all the time, He has been saying, "I created him, I don't need to remove anything to use him. Stop looking for what is considered 'normal and standard' and focus on my glory."

And the LORD said, "I will cause all my goodness to pass in front of you, and I will proclaim my name, the LORD, in your presence. I will have mercy on whom I will have mercy, and I will have compassion on whom I will have compassion. (Exod. 33:19)

How much time have I wasted? How much time have you wasted believing something has to be fixed, adjusted, modified, bigger, smaller, thinking all the *T*s have to be crossed and *I*s dotted before it can be used of God? This scripture shows God's almighty power and greatness. He can use all of His creations to bless His kingdom.

So who did it? Who was responsible for Miles's extra chromosome? God was. God did it! End of discussion.

CHAPTER 5

Ability to Impact

Thank you, Lord. It was not me. I'm not all that. I can have all the self-esteem I want, but I don't have the ability to create life; I only have the ability to bring it forth. What a shifting and lifting occurs when burdens are released and bonds of wrong thinking are loosed. Only God alone can do that. But I also realize that I can have great impact on Miles's life, positively or negatively. We, you and I, have the ability to be blessings to God's people. How? Through perfect and passionate obedience to God.

> If you fully obey the Lord your God and carefully follow all his commands I give you today, the Lord your God will set you high above all the nations on earth. All these blessings will come upon you and accompany you if you obey the Lord your God. (Deut. 28:1–2 NIV)

Not only will the blessings come but they will accompany me. This means they will go with, keep me, teach me, lead me, strengthen me, and take good care of me. The Lord's blessings can be active in our lives.

> You will be blessed in the city and blessed in the country. The fruit of your womb will be

blessed, and the crops of your land and the young of your livestock-the calves of your herds and the lambs of your flock. Your basket and your kneading trough will be blessed. 6. You will be blessed when you come in and blessed when you go out. (Deut. 28:3–6 NIV)

Oh yes, we read it correctly. With obedience comes strong assurance and confidence. I have the ability to bring curses or blessings upon Miles's life. So I need to know my role. I could not create him, but I sure can affect him. I can help or hinder. I can help or discourage. Oh, thank you, God, for your Word right now. Thank you, Holy Spirit.

The Lord will grant that the enemies who rise up against you will be defeated before you. They will come at you from one direction but flee from you in seven. The Lord will send a blessing on your barns and on everything you put your hand to. The Lord your God will bless you in the land he is giving you. The Lord will establish you as his holy people, as he promised you on oath, if you keep the commands of the Lord your God and walk in his ways. Then all the peoples on earth will see that you are called by the name of the Lord, and they will fear you. The Lord will grant you abundant prosperity—in the fruit of your womb, the young of your livestock and the crops of your ground—in the land he swore to your forefathers to give you. The Lord will open the heavens and the storehouses of his bounty, to send rain on your land in due season and to bless all the works of your hands. You will lend to many nations but will borrow from none. The Lord will make you the head, not the tail. If you pay attention to the commands of the Lord your God that I give you this day and carefully follow them, you will always be at the top, never at the bottom. Do not turn aside from any of the commands I give you today, to the right or to the left, following other gods and serving them. (Deut. 28:7–14 NIV)

It is so clear now; it had been so foggy for a while. I rebuke you Satan in the name of the Lord my God. True obedience will always lead to blessings in due season. It will always lead to peace. It provides the "I know that I know that I know." Miles will always be taken care of. Oh, if I just do my part, if I run this race with grace, if I seek His face, if I hear and do what the Word says, I can be a blessing to Miles.

CHAPTER 6

Healing the "Issue"

So I have my foundation. God made all of us, and He can work through us just as we are. I, for the most part, rest well in this knowledge. But God does heal. The Bible clearly states,

> Having said this, he spit on the ground, made some mud with saliva, and put it on the man's eyes. Go, he told him, wash in the Pool of Siloam. So the man went and washed, and came home seeing. (John 9:6–7)

> And the Lord will take away from thee all sickness, and will put none of the evil diseases of Egypt, which thou knowest, upon thee; but will lay them upon all them that hate thee. (Deut. 7:15)

> He said to her, "Daughter, your faith has healed you. Go in peace and be freed from your suffering." (Mark 5:34)

There was a time that I would beg, miss time from work, or miss a bill to gain a healing for my son. During the first year, I researched medicines that claim to help children with Down syndrome all while praising God and thanking him for all that He is. I purchased one product, and it did not produce the *miracle* that I was looking for; it just made Miles constipated (LOL).

I was looking for a cure. I still believed that God loved me, but I was trying to make something happen. My faith was weak. Well, you may say nonexistent.

> Many are the plans in a man's heart, but it is the LORD's purpose that prevails. (Prov. 19:21)

But what's wrong with looking for cure?

> And a woman was there who had been subject to bleeding for twelve years, but no one could heal her. She came up behind him and touched the edge of his cloak, and immediately her bleeding stopped. 'Who touched me?' Jesus asked. When they all denied it, Peter said, 'Master, the people are crowding and pressing against you.' But Jesus said, 'Someone touched me; I know that power has gone out from me.' Then the woman, seeing that she could not go unnoticed, came trembling and fell at his feet. In the presence of all the people, she told why she had touched him and how she had been instantly healed. Then he said to her, 'Daughter, your faith has healed you. Go in peace.'" (Luke 8:43–48)

Maybe the inability to be cured is the blessing.

> To keep me from becoming conceited because of these surpassingly great revelations, there was given me a thorn in my flesh, a messenger of Satan, to torment me. Three times I pleaded with the Lord to take it away from me. But he said to me, "My grace is sufficient for you, for my power is made perfect in weakness." Therefore I will boast

all the more gladly about my weaknesses, so that Christ's power may rest on me. That is why, for Christ's sake, I delight in weaknesses, in insults, in hardships, in persecutions, in difficulties. For when I am weak, then I am strong. (2 Cor. 12:7–10)

Well, the obvious, which was not so obvious when the devil had given me sunshades so dark that I was blinded, is the "issue." This example in Luke above clearly indicates that while this woman may have tried other things first, she ultimately found the healing with God. However, she had the issue twelve years before the healing came. But immediately after she was able to interact with God, the problem that she had vanished. Here is where I am. There are two positive ways that I can choose to position Miles's "issue": (1) Miles does not have an issue. In Miles's mind, he does not have an issue. The issue is with my thinking, your thinking, and the world's thinking.

The extra chromosome is not an issue for Miles. Developing slowly or not being able to speak clearly is not an issue for Miles. The issue is with me and you. My issue is despair over dreams I had for him. People looking at him weird or with pity is the issue. Children not wanting to play with him is the issue.

The issues are not Miles's issues. The issues are with me and you. So the healing is not for Miles to receive. The healing is for me and you.

Thank you, God, right now for revelation. Miles does not need the healing. It is us that need healing. It is me. Healing from thinking I know what a *good life* looks like. Healing from a sense of embarrassment because my child can't do this and my child can't do that. Once I'm healed, the "issue" will be removed.

Heal those who are sick. (Matt. 10:8)

Miles is not sick. I'm the sick one. Sick with the cares and concerns of this world. Sick with selfishness about what I want my son to be able to do. Miles has a better health report than I do.

So why is Miles not healed? Miles is not sick. He does not have an issue.

(2) Miles's Down syndrome keeps us on our knees. We are forever humbled by knowing that we can't control everything. We had planned Miles's birth, taken prenatal vitamins, and read the books. But Miles was still born with an extra chromosome. However, his special need is for him; it makes him who he is. We need to pray for understanding of God's design. The fact is that everyone is God's creation.

Nonhealing and healing situations can impact the observers in the same way that they can the receivers. In a healing situation, we know that God is still in the miracle business. In a nonhealing situation, we see that God can operate through whatever the situation is. So there are no winners and losers. If God heals, great. If He does not, then let Him use you as you are. We can't let Satan fool us into keeping us frozen and unproductive because we did not get what we want in the way we wanted it. Move forward just as you are. Whatever changes God needs to make, He will, or He will use us as we are. Our ability to move forward and succeed in spite of our weaknesses can be a testimony for others. A person who is stuck in guilt and shame can see how the Lord moves on our behalf and be encouraged that God can do the same for them.

I know that a lack of faith can hinder the move of God. But I also know that when I did not have the knowledge of Him, when I had the knowledge but did not follow His words, when faith was my mother's speech and not my own, He still kept me. So I'm just foolish enough to believe that if He cared for me even when I turned my back on Him, disrespected Him, and sinned with no thought of repenting, and now that I've decided to live for Him and Him alone, He will not let me go. I'm looking ahead and moving forward.

> Brothers, I do not consider myself yet to have taken hold of it. But one thing I do: Forgetting what is behind and straining toward what is ahead, I press on toward the goal to win the prize for which God has called me heavenward in Christ Jesus. (Phil. 3:13–14)

CHAPTER 7

Who Is My Brother's Keeper?

Parents, whether dealing with a child with special needs or not, especially through age eighteen and sometimes beyond, have thoughts like "What will happen to them if I'm not around?" "Who will take care of them?" or "Will they be alright?" This is essentially magnified within me. Early on, it was all consuming. I thought about TV shows I had seen and newspaper articles I had read about people in group homes and mental facilities being abused. This tore my heart. When I die, who will take care of him? Where will he live? People are going to take advantage of him. Who is going to protect him? I won't be around forever. Who will be Miles's keeper?

> Now Cain said to his brother Abel, "Let's go out to the field." And while they were in the field, Cain attacked his brother Abel and killed him. Then the Lord said to Cain, "Where is your brother Abel?" "I don't know," he replied, "Am I my brother's keeper?" (Gen. 4:8–9)

> So when the Midianite merchants came by, his brothers pulled Joseph up out of the cistern and sold him for twenty shekels of silver to the Ishmaelites, who took him to Egypt. (Gen. 37:28)

> When Esau heard his father's words, he
> burst out with a loud and bitter cry and said to
> his father, "Bless me—me too, my father." But
> he said, "Your brother came deceitfully and took
> your blessing." (Gen. 27:34–35)

I hope you know that the devil is:

- a work alcoholic
- committed to his position, committed to his cause
- volunteers for overtime
- will skip breaks and lunches
- does not spend time complaining about his job
- always employee of the month in his kingdom.

Yes, he will even attempt to use the living, breathing Word of God to distract us and shake our faith in God. Here I am concerned about Miles's welfare, and Satan reminds me of scriptures of families turned against each other. Blood against blood, taking the concern and the love I have for Miles and creating worry, doubt, and fear. Once we are consumed by fear, we will not be able to be effective in God's kingdom. We can't build, teach, guide, and grow because we can't MOVE!

Those events did happen in the Bible, but there is also instruction and guidance on how we are to treat one another. Cain, Joseph's brothers, and Jacob did not act as they should have. They were wrong. Why did I allow the devil to direct me toward bad examples, toward items that are not fuel for my life? Okay, I hear you, saints. Because that is what he does: simple manipulation. Twisting, turning, covering up, and hiding what will be strength for my soul. Moving me away from the light and into to the darkness. See, the Word of God also says,

> Your eyes have seen all that the Lord did in
> Egypt to Pharaoh, to all of his officials and to
> all his land. With your own eyes you saw that

those great trials, those miraculous signs and great wonders. But to this day the Lord has not given you a mind that understands or eyes that see or ears that hear. During the forty years that I led you thorough the desert, your clothes did not wear out, nor did the sandals on your feet. You ate no bread and drank no wine or other fermented drink. I did this so that you might know that I am the Lord your God. (Deut. 29:2–6)

Do nothing out of selfish ambition or vain conceit, but in humility consider others better than yourselves. Each of you should look not only to your own interests, but also to the interests of others. (Phil. 2:3–4)

Look at the birds of the air; they do not sow or reap or store away in barns, and yet your heavenly Father feeds them. Are you not much more valuable than they? Who of you by worrying can add a single hour to his life? (Matt. 6:26)

Here is evidence that God Himself takes care of us. He instructs us all on how we are to treat each other, and He reminds us of our relationship with Him. These scriptures are so bright and encouraging that I need sunshades. They bring light to my soul. They bring strength to my tired, aching mind. So I say, "Oh no, devil. God has got Miles, or shall I proclaim, God has got this!"

Early on, although I was not seeing it, God placed people in our lives that were concerned about Miles. I mean really concerned about Miles. Not in a manner of pity but in an encouraging way. Not only concerned but equipped. Yeah, let's stay there. If a roof is leaking and there is no God-given knowledge or skills on how to fix the roof, the roof will continue to leak.

His physician mentioned that he had about five or six other patients that he had cared for that had special needs. See, I thought that when he was speaking about Down syndrome, he was crazy, but what God had done was lead us to someone who was ready and able. Thank you, Lord! Oh, it was not by chance that we ended up with Dr. Stephen Bolduc. I'm not sure if you recall, but I had chosen him before Miles was born. Oh, let me back up. God had led us to him. I, at this very moment, can't even recall how I was led to him. Have you ever looked back and don't even know how you got through something, and you just looked up, and you were on the other side? God is so good!

God placed Alonza and Tanya Frazier in our lives, and I honestly don't remember how our friendship first began. But I recalled being so filled with gratitude when they made the drive from Newport News to Children's Hospital of the King's Daughter (CHKD) in Norfolk on more than one occasion when Miles had open heart surgery to bring us food. A drive, depending on traffic, that could easily be over an hour. I know now that God was expanding Miles's village for him and for us.

But it does not stop there. Remember all of the church members who came and prayed at the hospital? They were all involved in the educational system. Not just involved but worked in Human Resources (HR), administration, and had a special education background, already set to lead and guide us. Not only that, they had experiences and knowledge about what could be and what was possible and what was needed to set Miles up for success in the public school system. Another example of what we call divine appointment.

None of this was a coincidence. Their presence in our lives was to help us gain a better reality of what is and what is yet to come. Hope. They gave us hope.

As we moved and are moving on, especially as it relates to our family, extended families, friends, caregivers, teacher assistants, teachers, and administrators, it is so evident that while we are accountable as his parents, we are not the only concerned citizens; and as Philippians tells us above, we are not the only people with responsibility for Miles.

During one of the Newport News School Board Special Education Committee (SEAC) meetings, our chairperson, as she was acknowledging some teachers, indicated that unlike most parents, teachers chose to be in our children's lives. I was so struck by that thought. Miles was given to us, and we take full responsibility. We have a natural love for him. But people who choose to work with people with special needs, who think differently, who can't express themselves in what we deem *normal* manner, made a choice.

Choose is defined as:

- "to select from a number of possibilities; pick by preference"
- "to prefer or decide (to do something)"
- "to want; desire"

Oh, thank you, Lord. I just love you so. If we seek we will find. Why do we worry about the welfare of Miles and other people with special needs? God will place believers or nonbelievers in their lives that have a true love for them and a desire to serve and take care of them. God will place people in their paths, in their lives, that feel a sense of responsibility for them. They'll look after them.

People will look at other options, other career paths, paths that offer more money, more worldly prestige, but some CHOOSE to be in the lives of our children. Oh, how precious is that thought to me. God gives people a strong compassion and concern for people with special needs. So the choice may not be a choice after all. God placed the compassion and desire within them that leads them to Miles, to your child, your grandchild, your relative, your neighbor, and your friend with special needs.

To Satan, I say your schemes, your tricks, did not work. See, I have real life examples of "brother's keepers." I read the whole story.

Joseph:

"The Lord was with Joseph and he prospered." (Gen. 39:2)

Esau:

> But Esau said, "I already have plenty, my brother. Keep what you have for yourself." (Gen. 33:9)

In the matchless name of Jesus, I believe and accept that Miles will not want for anything, and no harm will ever come his way. Who is my son's keeper? God and all the Saints.

CHAPTER 8

Let YOUR Light Shine

> In the same way, let <u>your</u> light shine before men, that they may see your good deeds and praise your Father in heaven. (Matt. 5:16, emphasis added)

The "your" in the scripture above is an individual reference. I can't shine your light for you, and you can't shine my light for me.

Are you familiar with this scene that plays out with parents and grandparents? You ask one question about the child, and out comes a wallet full of pictures or a very proud comment about what the child is doing or has done. Early on, Satan planted a sense of, well, not really embarrassment but, awkwardness in conversations about my son. I could not say that Miles was walking at nine months; he was well over one year old before he began to walk. So in conversations about how children were doing, I did not really feel as if I could participate. I only commented if someone specifically asked. I was the parent without the pictures in the wallet. So was I embarrassed of my son? That's what the devil told me and it led to me carrying the heavy weight of shame.

Then one day, as a result of constant pressing toward a relationship with God, the light came on. As indicated in Matthew above, Miles has a light that needs to be shown so that people will come to know and praise God. We have received so many comments about how Miles's praise and worship during church service lifts the hearts of others. Sometimes I worry that he is out of order during church services. I have gotten looks from people. But more often than not, I receive words of encouragement and "Leave him alone. He's all right." That old devil would have you to believe that your child is a distraction, but in reality, your child could be a catalyst for someone's sense of compassion and ability to see the work of God's hands on the life of others.

I'm still not great at this one, but I do have a desire to have him become more socially integrated in our society. Not only for his sake but for others as well. He has danced with the Dance Ministry and played the drums at church. I heard comments like "About time" and "It was so nice to see him participate." Miles has a light, and I won't be responsible for covering it.

If you have a child with special needs, don't keep them hidden. Don't just have them in special education environments. Share them with the world. You may get some odd looks sometimes, but smile and keep pressing. Just like any other child, our children's self-esteem will be influenced by us. Don't make them feel like second-class citizens. The harder we push for inclusion, the sooner it will come. There have been a lot of strides in this area, but there is still work to do.

I mentioned earlier how Satan used *"developmentally delayed"* to shape my vision of my son. I hear *can't, weak, won't, never, slow,* and more with that classification. For years, it tortured me. Then, although I had read it a thousand of times and claimed it for my life, the scripture in Ecclesiastes 9:11 jumped into my spirit:

> I have seen something else under the sun:
> The race is not to the swift or the battle to the
> strong but he who endures to the end.

Simply put, Miles's delay does not mean he can't or won't. He has his own developmental timetable. Real joy is not always in how fast something is done. If someone faces adversity, overcomes obstacles and still achieves, wow, that is truly something special.

CHAPTER 9

His Name

Miles Elijah Harris

So there was a movie with Zakee Howze in it, *Mo' Better Blues*. His character's name was Miles in the movie. I liked it. I thought it was a strong name, a different name, and we settled on it. But now as I write, I can't recall why we chose Elijah exactly. I know we wanted to use a name from the Bible. A name that was positive and expressed our faith to show our desire for our son to have a blessed life. So without that memory, I researched Elijah to get a better understanding, hoping something would trigger the reason why we chose it.

Elijah is the Hebrew *Eliyahu* that means "my God is Yahweh." Elijah represents a believer in the Lord.

Now, if you know Miles, I could stop there. Miles has no inhibitions. See, that is a part of his "difference." He feels and he does. It is not always proper and politically correct; but think about how much more impactful we could be in God's kingdom if we did not always stop to think about what people are saying, what they are thinking, what they will think, and simply not look at their faces. So he praises God for himself.

I recall the time when a teacher was sharing with me that Miles was not having such a good day. She took Miles to the timeout area. She was a believer and knew that prayer changes things. So she began to pray quietly, very quietly, as we know prayer is not allowed in

41

schools. As she prayed, she said Miles began to say hallelujah so loudly that she had to quiet him down as she was concern that her prayer would be discovered. Before she walked me through that moment, she asked, "Do you all go to church?"

So I thank God for no inhibitions with Miles. I thank God that Miles has knowledge of God and is not hesitant in showing praise for Him. Yes, I said knowledge of God. Miles's level of understanding is not aligned with ours, but say a prayer, sing a song, and you'll be amazed at the correct placements of his hallelujahs.

> Now Elijah, the Tishbite, from Tishbe in Gilead, said to Ahab, "As the Lord, the God of Israel, lives, whom I serve." (1 Kings 17:1)

Elijah was sent by the Lord. He showed up and immediately exclaimed who he served. He was a believer in God.

Miles ELIJAH Harris has a relationship with God today. What's in a name? What's in his name? His petition that he knows the Lord. I imagine him saying, "Mommy, stop worrying. God is my Lord, and I will serve Him in my own way." I hear you, Miles. I hear you now.

CHAPTER 10

It Is Not Blind Faith

Satan tried and continues to attempt to put thoughts in my mind that will lead me down a path where I only feel overwhelmed, ill-equipped, and hopeless, even twisting the Word of God and His guidance.

In one of my journaling moments for this book, I began to write about the difficulties of having blind faith. I wrote that not only is it difficult to obtain because once you have it, it is even more challenging to maintain. (I really was not trying to rhyme.) See Satan has been beating me down for years with the inconsistencies with my faith walk. Sometimes I get in a place where the guilt is gone, the worry is gone, and I'm confident that God has Miles in His hands. Then other times, I get very low—it probably could be defined as clinically depressed at times. Satan then rises up and says, "Look at you. If you had stronger faith in God, your head would not be bowed down. You are displeasing to God."

> And without faith it is impossible to please God, because anyone who comes to him must believe that he exists and that he rewards those who earnestly seek him. (Heb. 11:6)

He brings this verse to my remembrance and asks, "Where is your blind faith?" Thus, as I wrote this book, I had a desire to encourage you about seeking out your blind faith and placing it as a beacon for this journey of life that we are on. But then one day, I was quiet enough to allow myself to hear God's voice. "Blind faith?" my spirit began to say. "That is not the Word of God."

Faith has been defined as "unflagging trust and belief without firm proof." *Blind* has been defined as "sightless and unseeing." *Blindly* has a definition of "wildly, frantically, carelessly, recklessly, and aimlessly." Where in the Bible are we encouraged to have blind faith? Where does God instruct us to move about frantically, carelessly, and without clear direction? It does not. It says,

> Now faith is the substance of things hoped
> for, the evidence of things not seen. (Heb. 11:1)

> But since we belong to the day, let us be
> self-controlled, putting on faith and love as a
> breastplate, and the hope of salvation as a helmet.
> (1 Thess. 5:8)

> Like a city whose walls are broken down is a
> man who lacks self-control. (Prov. 25:28)

We are encouraged to have self-control. We are not called to live in a frantic state, running around like a chicken with its head cut off.

God never required blind faith. Let's look at the birth to toddler stages of life. The baby girl says in her mind, "She changed my diaper the last time I did not smell so good, so I'm confident she'll change me now." The baby relies on our track record and as a result will do number two, as we say, without even blinking. The baby gained faith that when **X** occurs, **Y** will occur.

That is the faith of the Bible. I know that if I serve Him, He will take care of me. I know that if I stay in His word, I will be strengthened and experience wonderful growth. I know all of this because of God's track record in my life.

> So if you faithfully obey the commands I
> am giving you today—to love the LORD your

44

> God and to serve him with all your heart and
> with all your soul—then I will send rain on your
> land in its season, both autumn and spring rains,
> so that you may gather in your grain, new wine
> and oil. (Deut. 11:13–14)

We all exercise faith every day. But Satan tries to make the faith of the Bible seem so different and difficult. It is not. Minister Zarlie Williams, who has passed from this life, one night in a Bible study, described faith like this: You work then you get paid. You have faith, based on what someone told you, that after the work has been completed, you will get paid at some point in the future. This is a display of faith as that future could be two or four weeks away. But we just trust and go to work.

> By faith the people passed through the Red
> Sea as on dry land; but when the Egyptians tried
> to do so, they were drowned. By faith the walls of
> Jericho fell, after the people had marched around
> them for seven days. By faith the prostitute
> Rahab, because she welcomed the spies, was not
> killed with those who were disobedient. (Heb.
> 11:29–31)

Faith is the belief that **X** will happen. It does not rely on what currently exists in the situation before **X** happens. The Red Sea had not parted before. Faith simply said he will provide a way of escape, not sure of what it will look like. But **X** will occur.

I had to stop allowing Satan to make me feel that I was too weak to have faith. I had to stop allowing him to get me to participate in mental debates about the fact that **X** has not occurred, or that it does not look like I wanted it to. My faith is in the fact that God created Miles, and He will take care of him. Period.

> Therefore be clear minded and self-con-
> trolled so that you can pray. (1 Pet. 4:7)

This verse speaks to the fact that being frantic and wild will negatively impact our communication with God. Prayer requires focus. Faith requires focus.

One night, Sydney, my daughter, was getting into bed; and when I turned off the light, she became fearful and said, "No, don't turn it off." She was afraid of the dark, only finding true comfort when the light was on. Yes, yes, yes! We are the same way. Once we read God's Word and gain truth, we move into the light.

> Jesus answered, "It is written: 'Man does not live on bread alone, but on every word that comes from the mouth of God." (Matt. 4:4)

The Bible is an instructional manual. It instructs us on all matters of life. It tells us how we should live and instructs us on how not to live. It is not a guessing game. It is not a blind faith walk. It gives complete and explicit directions on how we are to live.

> Therefore be clear minded and self-controlled so that you can pray. Above all, love each other deeply, because love covers over a multitude of sins. Offer hospitality to one another without grumbling. Each one should use whatever gift he has received to serve others, faithfully administering God's grace in its various forms. If anyone speaks, he should do it as one speaking the very words of God. If anyone serves, he should do it with the strength God provides, so that in all things God may be praised through Jesus Christ. (1 Pet. 4:7–11)

> Be imitators of God, therefore, as dearly loved children and live a life of love, just as Christ loved us and gave himself up for us as a fragrant offering and sacrifice to God. (Ephesians 5:1–2)

In addition to all this, take up the shield of
faith, with which you can extinguish all the flam-
ing arrows of the evil one. (Eph. 6:16)

God's word can be a shield and light against the darkness that
attempts to overtake our minds and hearts, if we let it.

CHAPTER 11

God's Plan

> But I have raised you up for this very pur-
> pose, that I might show you my power and that
> my name might be proclaimed in all the earth.
> (Exod. 9:16)

"I have raised you up" may refer to a vertical raise or a specific position. But "show you my power" signifies that our ability, skills, and so-called power don't compare. I know that with Miles and other people with disabilities, we often get amazed at their abilities. Why? Because we spend so much time focusing on what they can't do. I remember early on, after Miles's diagnosis, we went to a genetic counselor, and her message was constant: he won't do that, he can't do this, he will experience this, he won't experience that. I wanted to scream at one point. Here I am with a less than a six-week old baby, trying to process her telling me that he will never drive. Really? Excuse me, I'm still learning how to burp him.

Why don't we use that same set of glasses when we are considering people without a special need? I'm about five feet and four inches tall. I did not grow up with people saying she will never be able to dunk a basketball. She will never be able to reach that item without standing in a chair. No, I, like a great majority of people, lived life focusing effort on what I did well. If there were skills needed in a certain area, I worked to develop them more. So it should be with our children with special needs. Focus on what is, not what isn't. Because just like with us so-called people without disabilities, when there is an isn't or a can't, if we move up and let God, He will make a way. He will provide. He will raise us up. He raises us all up.

Miles is special because God's power is magnified through him. Wow, Miles knows the words to the song. Wow, Miles can put his clothes on by himself. Wow, Miles can turn on and play the Wii by himself. It is so nice to have such a visible view, all the time, of God's hands moving in Miles's life.

> The Lord foils the plans of the nation; he
> thwarts the purposes of the peoples. (Ps. 33:10)

> Many are the plans in a man's heart, but it
> is the LORD's purpose that prevails. (Prov. 19:21)

I remember, as I rubbed my growing stomach, I thought about what I wanted him to be. Then I recall asking myself the things that were going through Andre's head after the diagnosis of Down's. I felt bad that his dreams of how he would interact with his son were forever changed. My heart was hurting for a loss of something that we never even had. Andre was so happy, looking forward to being a daddy and determined to be a good one. Now what would he do? We even had another interaction with an agency that indicated that marriages were often broken over the stress of raising a child with a disability. I became stressed and was filled with worry all the time, in complete fear of the unknown. This entire situation was not what we had planned.

> Trust in the LORD with all thine heart; and
> lean not unto thine own understanding. In all
> thy ways acknowledge him, and he shall direct
> thy paths. (Proverbs 3:5–6)

> Many are the plans in the mind of a man,
> but it is the purpose of the LORD that will stand.
> (Proverbs 19:21)

So what did Andre do? He did what any great father would do. He has doted on Miles from day one. He has loved and cared for Miles in such a tender way. In a way that makes me fall in love with him over and over again when I witness his care and love for Miles. His love for Miles has blinded him to any concern about Miles's differences or what he can't do. He is proud of Miles. Simply put, he just loves him. Andre did what all parents are instructed to do.

> I am God, and there is no other; I am God,
> and there is none like me. I make known the end
> from the beginning, from ancient times, what is
> still to come. I say: My purpose will stand, and I
> will do all that I please. From the east I summon
> a bird of prey; from a far off land, a man to fulfill
> my purpose. What I have said, that will I bring
> about; what I have planned, that will I do. (Isa.
> 46:9–11)

God creates for a purpose. All of our lives have purpose. The ability for us to rise above our failures and come out of shame is for a purpose. Miles and other people with or without special needs have been authored by the same great God. There is no set of persons that is greater than the other. God has a plan for the life of people with disabilities just as He does for people without disabilities.

To those of us who don't call ourselves people with special needs, we are not all that and a bag of chips. People are people, and God is God.

> "Before I formed you in the womb, I knew
> you." (Jer. 1:5)

Train up a child in the way he should go,
And when he is old he will not depart from it.
(Proverbs 22:6)

Discipline your children, and they will give
you peace of mind and will make your heart glad.
(Proverbs 29:17)

There is a purpose inside each and every one of us. If we submit ourselves to God, He will equip and prepare us to do our assigned work for the kingdom.

God is speaking to everyone in this verse, people without disabilities and people with disabilities.

To the parent of a child with special needs, to the sibling of a child with special needs, to the aunt, uncles, cousins of a child with special needs, to the teacher, to the bus driver, to the stranger that sees a child with special needs, God made them just like He made you and me. There are no mistakes in God. Let's stop worrying about their *needs*, let's just LOVE them.

Thank you God for leading me to your truth. I'm so grateful to you for allowing me to be Miles's mother. I also thank you for the person reading this book. Please keep your grace and mercy upon them and their family. Thank you Lord for your faithfulness toward me!

ABOUT THE AUTHOR

Chenelle and Andre Harris live in Hampton Roads, Virginia with their two children, Miles and Sydney. Chenelle maintains an encouragement blog, www.walkinthetruth.com. She believes that everyone has wonderful purpose and potential inside of them. Her prayer is that this book will lift up a bowed down head, mend a broken heart, make someone smile, provide strength, encourage, and/or heal a broken spirit.

9 781636 304571